BRIDGNORTH
A Pictorial History

An aquatint by Paul Sandby in 1784, showing drastic repairs underway on the bridge whilst the riverfolk continue their bustling activities.

BRIDGNORTH
A Pictorial History

Margaret Rutter
& Heather Dent

Phillimore

1998

Published by
PHILLIMORE & CO. LTD.,
Shopwyke Manor Barn, Chichester, West Sussex

ISBN 0 85033 944 8

Printed and bound in Great Britain by
BIDDLES LTD.
Guildford, Surrey

List of Illustrations

Frontispiece: The Bridge by Paul Sandby, 1784

Acknowledgements

We gratefully acknowledge the sponsorship of Lawson Mardon Star Ltd.

We are also indebted to Dr. Malcolm Wanklyn of Wolverhampton University, who guided us throughout, Bridgnorth Public Library, who gave us a base, and Shrewsbury College of Art and Technology (Bridgnorth Campus), who provided darkroom facilities.

Over 50 of the illustrations are printed from glass plates, many of which were rescued from Bridgnorth tip by Walter Rutter: 8, 11, 14, 18, 24, 32, 43, 47, 49, 51, 53, 58, 60, 62, 64, 65, 66, 68, 71, 74, 77, 79, 81, 86, 89, 92, 95, 97, 98, 105-9, 111, 113, 120, 121, 122, 125, 126, 127, 134, 135, 140, 141, 143, 144, 146, 147, 148, 150, 151, 155, 156, 157, 159.

Other illustrations are reproduced by kind permission of: Mrs. R. Bailey, 13; Bridgnorth Civic Society, 83; Bridgnorth Library, 5, 6, 9, 12, 17, 26, 27, 29, 44, 61, 124; Della Copeland, 88; Muriel Davies, 37; Heather Dent, 96, 110; Julie Dent, 78; Mary Geraghty, cover, 101; Len Hand, 130; John Hare, 30, 54, 56, 94; Natalie Hodgson, 46; David Jennings, 38, 39, 40; Ministry of Defence, 2; Edith Oliver, 131; Geoff Parfitt, 115, 116, 117, 149; Margaret Rutter, 4, 7, 10, 16, 19, 22, 25, 28, 31, 33, 34, 35, 41, 42, 45, 48, 50, 52, 55, 57, 57, 59, 63, 67, 69, 70, 72, 73, 75, 80, 84, 85, 90, 91, 99, 100, 102, 103, 104, 112, 114, 118, 128, 129, 132, 133, 136, 137, 138, 142, 152, 153, 158, 160-163; Shropshire Record Office, 15, 139; Sylvia Stubbs and Roger Roden, 36, 82, 87, 93, 145, 154, 164-74; Robin Tench, 20, 21, 23, 76, 119, 123.

Peter Dent drew the maps, nos. 1 and 3.

Introduction

Approaching Bridgnorth from the east, the visitor suddenly comes upon one of the most spectacular setting of any town in Britain.

Across the river Severn the medieval planned town is perched dramatically on its sandstone bluff, overlooking the terraced flood plains. Set against the backdrop of the Clee hills, the townscape is framed at each end of the skyline by the contrasting towers of the two parish churches of St Mary Magdalene and St Leonard's. Below these, tumbling haphazardly down the cliffs to the river are the cottages, winding lanes and flights of steps leading down to the bridge and remains of great warehouses, a silent tribute to Bridgnorth's national importance as an inland river port and boat building centre in earlier times.

The geology of Shropshire is a fascinating study, far too complicated to attempt more here than sketch in some of the influences which led to the establishing of Bridgnorth on its commanding site. The stretches of the Severn Valley, into which the town nestles, were formed approximately twenty thousand years ago when the last Ice Age altered the course of the river, pushing it over and eventually through the limestone ridge of Wenlock Edge, from where it gradually cut its way through the red sandstone plateaux of the western midlands. The ice itself travelled no further south than Eardington and eventually receded northwards as the climate grew warmer, but the subsequent quantities of meltwater have left successive flood terraces high above the river channel. The sandstone plateau through which the river flows is actually a series of fossilised sand dunes formed some 260 million years earlier in a region south of the equator with a climate similar to that of the Sahara desert today. The cross-bedded layers of fine-grained sand which had changed direction with the wind can be seen clearly in the exposed cliff faces within the town.

Permian sandstone of this type is soft and easy to burrow into and since man has always looked for dry, sheltered places to live in, these rocks have been utilised, especially along the exposed ridges of the eastern edge of the valley where there are remains of cave dwellings and a chapel. At a place known as the Hermitage, legend has it that Ethelward, brother of King Athelstan and grandson of Alfred the Great, spurned life at court and went into retreat in these caves. The caves were certainly lived in until the early years of the 20th century and to this day cottages built against the cliffs on the west bank have cave rooms and cellars.

Below the Hermitage ridge and largely hidden from view nestles the town's cemetery. Established in 1855, it is a place of outstanding beauty and tranquillity.

Transport and Communications

The river Severn has always been wild and its levels variable and during the Middle Ages it was navigable from Bristol up to and beyond the Welsh border. The use of coracles on the river was recorded in A.D. 60 and, as early as 1198, an entry in the accounts of the Sheriff of Shropshire refers to passenger traffic carried in wherries from Bridgnorth to Gloucester. By the 17th century flat-bottomed Severn trows or smaller barges, hauled first by men and later by horses, carried foreign spices, wines, sugar and tobacco upstream and, on return, were able to sail downstream carrying Shropshire cheese and Welsh cloth, agricultural goods, iron goods from Coalbrookdale, coal and bricks from Broseley, and pottery from Coalport. The river flow, however, was seasonal and the 'bow haulers' frequently had to spend a considerable time ashore when there was insufficient water for navigation. Colourful tales abound of the activities of this bunch of extraordinarily fit and active men as the number of thriving alehouses documented in all the river towns will testify. So renowned were these men for their strength and teamwork that they were regularly seen as a ready source of conscription in times of war. In 1755 General Whitmore raised the 53rd Foot (later the 1st Battalion, KSLI) at Bridgnorth from these men. In the mid-18th century the stretch of river between Buildwas and Bewdley was the busiest on the Severn, with only Broseley exceeding Bridgnorth's tally of 75 vessels owned within, and plying from, the town.

Many industries and trades grew up in the town around the river trade, boat-building being one of the most important of them, with two main boatyards operating during the 18th century. Listed by Rev. Richard Cornes in 1739 (then Minister of St Mary Magdalene) they were both situated on the west bank, one where the gas works was later built, and the other, the most important yard, that of William Oakes, on the west bank opposite the southern end of the Bylet. Oakes built the last trow in Bridgnorth in 1868, although pleasure boats continued to be built until 1908.

Other industries dependent on the river trade included tanning, malting and rope-making. The building of the canals was at first feared by the river folk, but in fact they led to an enhancement of trade, opening up channels of communication with Liverpool and the Mersey via Stourport. However, it was the building of the railways which tolled the final death knell for the river trade and the last trow to ply its trade, loaded with firebricks, sank ingloriously after hitting Bridgnorth bridge in 1895.

Roads have also played an important part in Bridgnorth's history, being situated close to the ancient route from Bristol to Chester and the old salt route from Droitwich into Wales. By the 18th century the town was within reach of London via Wolverhampton, Birmingham and Worcester. In the later middle ages Bridgnorth was considered the second most important borough in Shropshire and in 1763 was described as 'A place of great trade, both by land and water' with roads radiating outwards to the Welsh Marches and all the main Midland towns.

Saturdays and Mondays saw great numbers of carriers bringing people and goods in to the town for the markets.

The origin of the bridge itself provokes much debate: there was a bridge recorded at Cwatbryg (Quatbridge) in 896 and a burgh created on the east bank of the Severn at Quatford (where Earl Roger founded the collegiate church of St Mary Magdalene in 1086) is recorded in Domesday as a part of the village of Eardington (on the other side of the river, indicating a river crossing). Bridgnorth bridge dates at least from the early 13th century, the earliest known reference being 1272. A ford undoubtedly existed a few hundred feet downstream from the present bridge, using the Bylet and a rib of rock creating a shallow way diagonally across the river.

It is not known how long the bridge at Cwatbryg was in use. For a long period up until 1447, when the bridge was built at Bewdley, Bridgnorth was the only dry crossing place of the Severn between Worcester and Shrewsbury. Over the centuries the fabric of the bridge suffered greatly from flooding and the surviving records reveal detailed accounts of rebuilt arches, renewed stonework, widened carriageway and temporary wooden arches (as can be seen in the frontispiece). Tolls were levied in varying degrees to cover these costs until the mid-19th century. In 1823 John Smallman of Quatford made some major alterations, adding parapet railings and widening the roadway over the middle two arches, carrying it on cast-iron ribs. The latest major work was done on the bridge in 1960, when the entire roadway was widened and carried on 70-ft. long pre-stressed concrete beams cast by Tarmac of Wolverhampton. Uniform parapet railings were used between the existing stone pedestrian refuges.

Several busy roads now converge on Bridgnorth and in 1985 the long-awaited bypass bridge was built, relieving much of the pressure on the town's roads. However, by 1994, the amount of traffic crossing the town bridge was already in excess of pre-bypass figures!

Railway mania was sweeping the county in 1845-6 and the Severn valley attracted the attention of many surveyors and engineers, not least Robert Stephenson, but the bickerings between promoting companies and local land owners were so prolonged that it was 1862 before the Severn Valley line was finally opened, linking Hartlebury, near Kidderminster, to Bridgnorth and Shrewsbury via Ironbridge. By this time, however, the main national lines had already bypassed Bridgnorth and so Wolverhampton was the nearest main line station. Efforts were made to promote a line linking the two towns, but to no avail and when Dr. Beeching's axe fell on the Severn Valley branch line in 1963 the bridge and track leading northwards through the long tunnel under High Town was taken up, thus denying the successful present-day Severn Valley Railway Company the chance of reinstating the scenic route alongside the river to Shrewsbury. The remaining track running south to Kidderminster does, however, greatly add to the tourist aspect of the town and attracts steam enthusiasts from all over the country together with film and television companies who are always eager to use the natural 'sets' of Victorian and Edwardian England and the beautiful riverside scenery.

Town Roads and Steps

The first paths would have been cut into the rock face whilst the castle was being built, as access for materials and supplies from the river was vital. Seven flights of steps now ascend the cliff, in places cut 20 feet deep through the rock, and other short flights connect with the wharfage or climb the hill on the eastern bank. Later, as the port developed, it became necessary to draw larger loads up the hill but, until the building of New Road in 1786, the main route up to High Town from the bridge was the steep, winding Cartway.

By 1770 stage coaches were calling at High Street inns and the number of fine buildings in the town dating from this time suggests that Bridgnorth had become a very

The Articles of Surrender
Of BRIDGNORTH CASTLE

I. That all Commissioned Officers of horse, and all Captains of Foot, shall march away to any of His Majesty's Garrison or Armies within 40 miles, with their horses and arms for themselves, and each of them to have a servant with his horse and sword, and wearing Apparel. Free quarter for 30 miles, and safe conduct, and not to march less than 8 miles a day.

II. That all inferior Commisioned Officers shall have liberty to march with their swords, and all the common Soldiers without Arms, to any of his Majesty's Garrisons or Armies within 40 miles as before stated, or laying down their arms, to live at their own habitations for a fortnight, and afterwards to take the negative Oath if they live within the County, or letters from hence to the Committees of the several Counties, where they intend to reside, and to have passes granted accordingly.

III. That all Clergymen, Townsmen, and Countrymen, within the castle, may have liberty to repair to their own habitations, provided they lay down their Arms, and a fortnight's time allowed them for taking the negative Oath, and not to live within a mile of the Parliament Garrisons; or otherwise if they should desire it, to march to any of the King's Garrisons or Armies.

IV. That all the wounded and sick persons in the castle, shall have liberty to reside in the Low Town, or elsewhere, till they be fit to travel, and then to have passes to go home or to any of the King's Garrisons or Armies.

V. That Sir Robert Howard, Sir Vincent Corbet, Sir Edward Acton, and Sir Francis Ottley, with each of them their horses and Arms, and two men apiece, with their horses and Swords and their masters wearing Apparel, shall have liberty to march to their several habitations, and to continue there for the space of two months in which time they are to make their election whether they will go to make their peace with Parliament, or go beyond Sea or to any of the King's Garrisons or Armies, and to have passes accordingly; they engaging themselves to do nothing prejudicial to the Parliament in the meantime.

VI. That Mr. Howard, Mr. Fisher and Mr. Grovenor, shall march away with their Horses and Arms, with one man apiece, with their Apparel and Swords, to any place within 40 miles.

VII. The Lieutenant Colonel Hosier and Doctor Lewen shall march away without horse or Arms, to any of the King's Garrisons, or any other place within 30 miles, provided it be not within this County.

VIII. That Mr. Milward, Captain of the Garrison, may have liberty to go with a horse to his house at Leighton, in this County, and to take with him his manuscripts, and their to live, taking the negative Oath within one month's time, or is to march away out of the County with the rest.

IX. That the Clerks to the Commisioners, may have liberty to march as the rest of the inferior Officers, and to have the same conditions, and to take with them all papers concerning the Garrison, and their wearing Apparel.

X. That Lady Ottley, her children, and Maid servant, have liberty with their wearing Cloathes, to go to Pitchford, or the Hay, and there to live unmolested.

XI. That all women and Children within the castle, may have liberty to go to their own or any of their friends houses, provided it not be within a mile of this Garrison.

XII. That all Gentlemen, Officers, and Soldiers within the Castle, Strangers as well as others desiring to go beyond the sea, shall have passes accordingly, and letters to the Committees of their several Counties, to afford them the like conditions as to the Gentlemen of this County, upon the surrender of this Castle here granted.

XIII. That the Surgeon belonging to this Garrison, shall march away; and to have the same conditions as the inferior officers.

XIV. That the Gunners and Powdermen, with their mates, may march away as the rest of the Common Soldiers.

XV. That no violence, injury, or incivility, shall be offered to any who shall march out of this castle, must be protected in all things according to the tenor of these Articles, and that sufficient Hostages on both sides be given for the performance of all, and every, the matters here agreed upon.

XVI. That the Governor, and the rest of the Officers, shall do their utmost endeavors to prevent and preserve all the Ordinances, Arms, Ammunition, Victuals, Provisions, Goods, Bedding and all other Accommodations necessary and belonging to the castle other than what is allowed to be taken by the afforsaid articles, and all these safe and unspoiled, to be delivered up together with the Castle unto the Committee whom they shall appoint, and the Articles to be confirmed by the Governor.

XVII. That if these Articles be consented to, the Castle be surrendered by Seven of the clock tomorrow morning, and those who intend to march to Worcester, to quarter in the Low Town, or any other Town within 5 miles of the Garrison, upon the return of the trumpeter and Officer sent to Worcester, provided they come within two days.

XVIII. That if any officer, or Soldier shall in any way maliciously spoil his horse or Arms, or misdemean himself in his march, such misdemeanor shall not be extended further than upon the party offending, and upon they, justice shall be done according to the discipline of War.

XIX. That all Commisioned Officers certified by the Governor of the Castle, and upon his certificate be allowed to march accordingly; and that all troopers march away with their swords.

XX. That Mr. Edward Lathun be delivered to the mercy of Parliament.

The articles of surrender were signed in St. Mary Magdelene's Church on Sunday 26th April, 1646.
Sir Robert Howard, Sir Vincent Corbet, Sir Edward Acton and Sir Francis Ottley signed as Commisioners for the King.
Colonel Andrew Lloyd, Colonel Robert Clive and Robert Charleton signed as Commisioners for the Parliament.

Articles of Surrender drawn up by Cromwell and signed on 26 April 1646 in St Mary Magdalene's Church by Sir Robert Howard, Sir Vincent Corbet, Sir Edward Acton and Sir Francis Ottley for the King and Colonel Andrew Lloyd, Colonel Robert Clive and Robert Charleton for Parliament.

desirable place to live in and visit. Stage coaching had grown from a few scattered routes in 1750 to a national network by the 1780s. There were, in fact, three rival lines calling daily at the *Crown* or *Pig and Castle* from Liverpool and Cheltenham as well as coaches and carriers connecting to London via Wolverhampton, Birmingham and Worcester. By this time most of the castle walls had been destroyed and it was possible to build the 'New Road' winding round the southern end of the castle promontory and entering the town through the outer bailey, along what is now known as West Castle Street and then via the narrow portal of the former Postern gate into the High Street. After the building of the railway station in 1862, the steep lane, once known as New Town, which dropped on the western side of the town from Listley gate, was renamed Railway Street. It is now lined with attractive cottages whose gardens rise up at the back to meet the remains of the old town walls.

In 1892 another of Bridgnorth's special features was constructed, a funicular railway connecting the bridge with Castle Walk, for centuries a popular place to promenade and enjoy the superb views up and down the river. This railway, still in use, is yet another tourist attraction. Refurbishment of the stations at either end of the railway and the cars in Victorian style with smart blue and gold livery has been completed.

The Castle

Although there is no known pictorial representation of the castle, we have a very colourful image presented to us in documentary evidence of life and events here down the years.

It has never been established whether the Brug, Bridge or Cwatbryg referred to in early documents is Bridgnorth itself or Quatford, two miles to the south. The Danes certainly crossed the Severn in the locality and Lady Aethelfleda, daughter of Alfred the Great and widow of Aethelred, King of Mercia, is known to have built a series of burghs at strategic points, one being at Brug. After the Norman invasion, Roger de Montgomery, first Norman Earl of Shrewsbury, built himself a fortified house at Quatford and in 1086 founded and endowed a collegiate church there to St Mary Magdalene. In 1098 Robert de Bellesme succeeded his father as earl and was soon in open rebellion against King Henry I. The rocky outcrop further up the river from Quatford and on the west bank presented a more easily defensible position and in 1101 he moved his entourage to this site. According to the chronicler Florence of Worcester he 'in great haste strengthened the walls of Aethelfleda's fortress'. However, Robert's rebellion was short-lived and the king took the castle after a siege. The nearby Panpudding Hill was very probably used as a siege castle at this time and for subsequent sieges throughout th\e next few hundred years. The Shropshire Parliamentarians certainly used it in 1646. There was another rebellion in 1155, by Hugh de Mortimer of Wigmore against Henry II. Once more the castle was captured and returned to royal rule. During the Middle Ages, when the Welsh border was being defended, Bridgnorth Castle was one of the most strongly defended in the Marches and received frequent royal visits. The King's House, that is the royal apartments within the castle walls, were kept in good repair up to Henry VIII's time. By 1628, the castle and grounds had passed into the hands of William Whitmore of Apley, who owned much of the property in the town and it was he, in 1642, who placed the castle at the disposal of Charles I. In 1645 the Royalist forces were in retreat throughout the country. Bridgnorth was one of the two last castles in Shropshire to hold out against the Parliamentarians and a summons to surrender was received and refused by the castle's commander, Sir Robert Howard. On 31 March 1646 Parliamentary troops broke through the town's defences to the north and a great fight ensued in St Leonard's churchyard, where Colonel Billingsley was slain with many of his men. After their retreat to the castle, the Royalists bombarded St Leonard's Church which was being used as an arsenal by the Parliamentarians. The church (in which the timbers of the dismantled Guild Hall and New House had been stored) and much of the High Street were consumed by fire, leaving only those buildings on the corner of Waterloo Terrace and Postern Gate and nos.3 and 4 close to the Northgate. Behind the present frontages, like that of the *Swan*, much earlier timbers can be found, some bearing the marks of burning. The Royalists in the castle resisted for three weeks. Eventually the Parliamentarians tried another tactic. A Colonel Lavington, an engineer, was put in charge of digging a long tunnel, of almost 70 feet, into the cliff on the east side of Castle Hill and right under St Mary's Church. After receiving threats to blow up the garrison, the castle was surrendered on 26 April 1646. Some months later orders were given for the complete demolition of the castle, and all we see today is the remains of the Norman keep leaning at a preposterous angle and a few remnants of the walls around the town. The outer bailey was rebuilt as two streets converging on the site of the great gate at the northern end, which was not wholly demolished until 1821. In 1897 the castle grounds were given to the town as a public garden by Major Foster of Apley.

The Town

The earliest townsfolk lived within the bailey walls, but by the end of the 12th century the Marches were becoming more settled with increasing population and developing trade. Consequently, Bridgnorth, one of several planned towns laid out across the region at this time, developed a long wide street outside the north gate of the castle, aligned north to south, with a market place from which roughly parallel streets stretched westwards at right angles. A wooden pallisade and, later, a stone wall and dry moats (ditches) were built around the town (1250) but small suburbs grew up even outside these walls (Northgate, New Town and Little Brug). In 1157 the town was large and prosperous enough to be granted a charter by Henry II. Between 1215 and 1630 Bridgnorth was in receipt of a long series of grants from successive monarchs giving trading advantages, the right to hold fairs. It was also privileged to charge tolls for the upkeep of the castle walls and bridge. Medieval planned towns were designed as trading centres usually established by the local lord who would then rent out space to traders. Shops with narrow frontages lined the streets, with long thin burgage plots running back behind them, allowing burgesses the necessary land to grow produce for sale or set up workshops for manufacturing goods. Careful examination of old maps showing these plots suggests that the original town 'without the walls' consisted, at first, of just the High Street up to the present position of the Town Hall with a large cattle market to the west bounded by St Mary's Street. The topography of the town still reveals the existence of many of these plots, although some have been levelled for car parks, and many small cottages and workshops remain hidden from view. Figure 2, the aerial photograph, clearly shows these plots.

Regular markets and four annual fairs brought trade by road from the surrounding agricultural land and by river from towns both upstream and downstream. There is still a cattle market, although it is now held at Tasley one mile to the west of the town, and each Saturday there is a colourful market lining the High Street and under the Town Hall where local folk sell their wares. In 1855 an elaborate Italianate market hall was built to move these traders from the street, but they resolutely refused to move their pitches!

On the eastern side of the High Street some of the shops sport awnings and pro-jections built out onto the pavement. These are the relics of 'piazzas' (covered walk-ways to provide some shelter and additional space for market stalls) which extended along the southern end of this side and at the northern end of the west side by Whitburn Street. In 1600 a High Cross existed at the junction of High Street and St Mary's Street close to the 'New House' (a stilted hall on the site of the present Town Hall). The town was so impoverished by the Civil War that appeals were made to Parliament for assistance in building a new town hall. The timbers on the upper floor of the present town hall came from a barn demolished at Much Wenlock and the supporting arches are of sandstone, later encased with brick. A brand new town hall was planned in the early 19th century, but fortunately the newly reformed Town Council had other matters to attend to at the time so Bridgnorth retained its picturesque High Street.

Churches

The first church, that dedicated to St Mary Magdalene, was built in 1101 inside the castle bailey, close to where the present one now stands. A late medieval church was replaced in 1792 with a building designed by the engineer Thomas Telford. In order to enhance the front elevation aspect, he orientated the church unusually, with the altar at the south end and the nave running northwards to its classical portico opening on to the fashionable East Castle Street. St Leonard's Church, built before 1200, of local sandstone and therefore subject to considerable erosion, has been successively repaired and rebuilt over the centuries. The existing building dates from 1862, but the cost of continual repair eventually proved too great and by 1978 it was decided to declare the church redundant. The building, still standing in its cathedral-like close, on the highest land in the town, is now used for occasional services and concerts and in 1993 became the venue for the annual English Haydn Festival.

Several other religious establishments have found a place in the town over the centuries. A hospital dedicated to the Virgin and St John was founded between 1179 in 1195 for the use of travellers and the Hospital of St James in 1224 for the sick and, particularly, the leprous of the town. Both were situated on the east bank of the river and have long disappeared, but they give their names to streets in the area. By 1244 a house for the Grey or Franciscan Friars had been founded on the west bank below St Leonard's Church. Excavations have shown this to have been a considerable establishment for a movement which spurned wealth. At the dissolution in 1535, the friars, who had also conducted services in St Osyth's Chapel on the bridge, were disbanded and parts of the friary became in turn a gentleman's house, an ale house, a malt house, part of a boat yard and a warehouse of the Southwell's carpet works. When the new housing development started on the site, the building developer, Bovis, allowed excavations to be made and ruins on part of the site are now preserved.

The Roman Catholic population of the 17th and 18th centuries in Bridgnorth was very small indeed before the Catholic Emancipation Act of 1829. Freedom to worship led to a growth in congregations and in 1856 St John's Roman Catholic Church was built on land given by Sir John Acton. It was rebuilt in its present form in 1896. Presbyterianism (now Independent) stems from the activities of Andrew Tristram, an associate of Richard Baxter. He was minister from 1656. Ejected from his living in Charles II's purge of Nonconformists in 1662, he is recorded in 1672 as being back in Bridgnorth licensed as a Presbyterian preacher at a house in the High Street. The Bridgnorth Independent congregation had their first meeting house on Stoneway steps in 1709, replaced by the present building in 1829. Later it became the Theatre-on-the-Steps. There was a Baptist society in the town by 1652 and in 1663 both Baptist and Presbyterian meetings were reported to the Government. Richard Synge, one of the Aldermen ejected in 1662, was probably a Baptist. His grandson John was a Baptist preacher and he and his descendants were the great pillars of this congregation in the 18th and 19th centuries. In 1704 the first Baptist chapel was built in West Castle Street and replaced by the present one in 1842. Wesleyan Society's places of worship were Mill Street, Bernard's Hill, St Mary's Steps and, finally, Cartway in 1854. A great merger took place in 1962 when the Methodist, Primitive Methodist and Congregational churches came together as the United Reformed Church and worshipped in the Cartway chapel.

Industry

Bridgnorth's craftsmen, as in most small market towns, produced mostly necessary items sufficient for their own use and for the inhabitants of the surrounding villages. However, they did provide some goods for a wider market. During the 18th century woollen cloth called 'frieze' which was thick and shaggy, was spun and woven in many private dwellings and transported by road. Large quantities of malt were also produced in the town and transported by river. The *Shropshire Gazetteer* of 1824 refers to 'An immense quantity of most excellent malt equal if not superior to any in the kingdom' and praises the production of barley on the western side of the river.

The Industrial Revolution within the Severn Gorge had an early impact on Bridgnorth. By 1802 Richard Trevithick was producing work at the Hazeldine foundry on the east bank where John Rastrick also played an important role. Steam engines were built for dredging, threshing and pumping and many were transported to Cornwall in particular and, of course, used locally. In 1814 a cargo for Lima, especially suited to the high altitude silver mines, left Bridgnorth: four pumping engines, four winding engines, an ore grinding mill and a rolling mill. It was taken by barge down the river and transhipped at Portsmouth. After they had been successfully set up, Trevithick sailed for Peru hoping for more orders, but none transpired. Hazeldine's foundry continued until 1830 when the firm became bankrupt. Bridgnorth played no further significant part in the heavy side of the Industrial Revolution.

Carpet weaving, which had begun as a cottage industry, notably in Cartway before 1780, developed into a very successful industry which was to dominate the local economy for 150 years. Joseph McMichael had set up the first carpet factory in Listley Street at the turn of the century and by 1842 there were three factories: McMichael's, Elcock's and Southwell's. Southwell's, built in 1824 on the site of the old friary, expanded rapidly and provided much needed employment as by this time the river trade had declined. The firm employed as many as 600 by the mid-19th century. In 1897 the firm manufactured a carpet presented by the Ladies of England to Queen Victoria on the occasion of her Diamond Jubilee. At the close of the First World War a Victory carpet was also presented to the Palace. The firm continued producing carpets until 1987 with a break during the Second World War when it went over to war work with Rootes, manufacturing aircraft components. In 1938 W.L. Southwell had retired and the business became an outpost of the Kidderminster industry. In the latter years only chenille and rubber-backed carpets were produced. The factory was demolished in 1988, allowing the remains of the old friary to be excavated and exposed. No other industry of any size developed, the railway arrived late and then only single track, providing no real link with the Black Country, which had largely taken over the industry of the Ironbridge Gorge. During the Second World War the Radio Development Company took over the Pale Meadow works in Hospital Street and continued to produce radio, television and electronic equipment until Decca took over the works in the early 1960s. Tatung, another electronics company, also established itself there briefly, but sadly the lure of rate-free space in the Telford Development area tempted them and many other firms away. Currently, by far the largest single employer in Bridgnorth is Lawson Mardon Star which manufactures aluminium foil products.

During the war an RAF camp was set up at Stanmore on the eastern ridge of the town and from then until its disbandment in 1963 almost every young Air Force conscript spend part of his training period in Bridgnorth. Now several small industries have developed in the industrial estate on the site.

Since the 1940s Bridgnorth's population has increased and large housing developments have mushroomed on the once green fields around the town. Many people travel to Telford or the West Midland conurbation to work and shop and great efforts have been made to develop the tourist attractions. With such an attractive townscape, the Severn Valley Railway, its proximity to the Ironbridge Gorge and all the beautiful walking country to the west, Bridgnorth looks set to succeed in this respect.

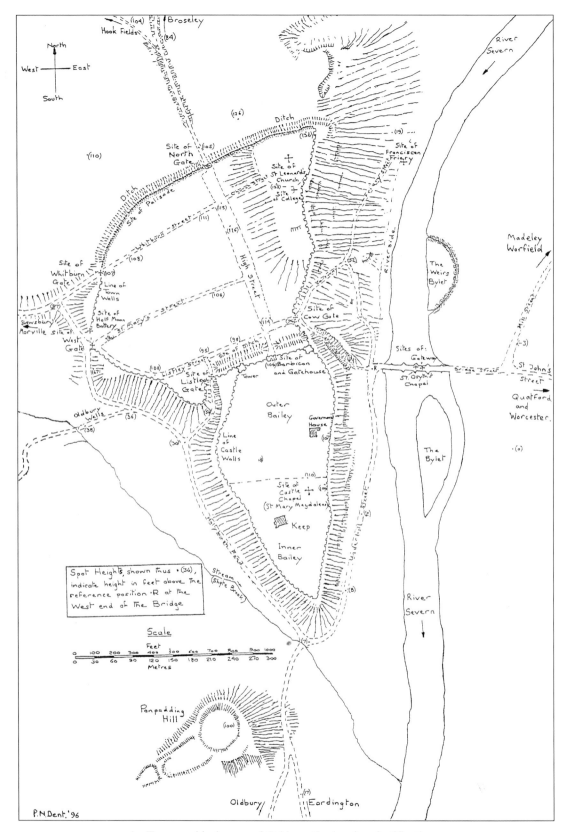

1 Topographical map of Bridgnorth showing fortifications.

2 This aerial photograph of 1948 graphically shows the topography of the town, with the pre-eminence of the castle site rising steeply up from the Severn. Panpudding hill stands out clearly bottom left of the picture, while the faint outline of the north bylet can just be seen silted up north east of the bridge. (Crown Copyright, 1948.)

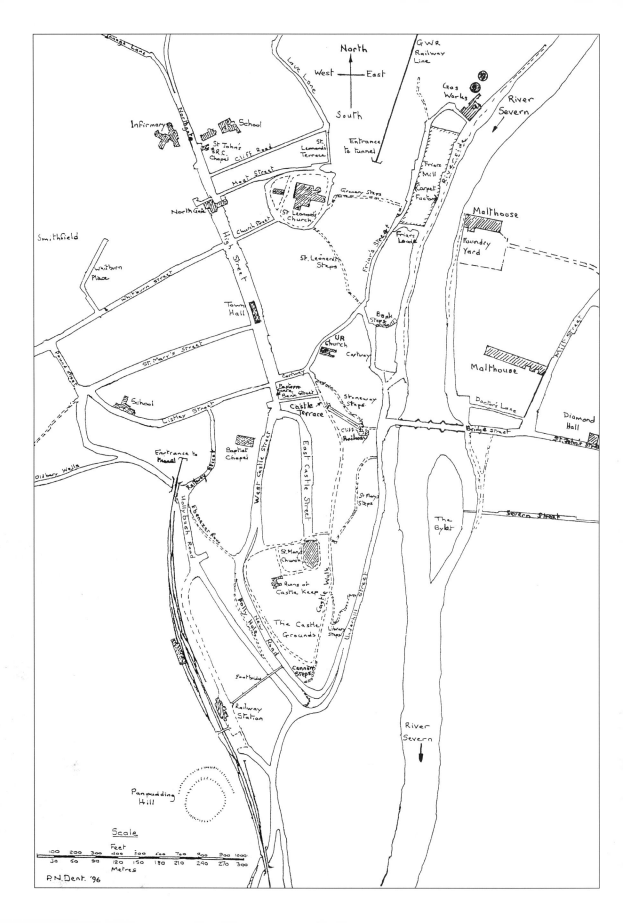

3 Town map of Bridgnorth, 1948.

4 Lithograph published by C. Edkins. Looking south from the High Rock, 1860: on the left, the Pale Meadow works built in 1835 for the production of carpets was by this time a spinning mill. Beneath the rock, Fort Pendlestone was also a spinning mill. It is described in the *Victoria County History* as 'a red sandstone castellated structure built in 1845 by Thomas Whitmore, the squire of Apley, on the site of the Old Town Mills, given by Henry III in 1227 under the great seal to the burgesses and their heirs for ever, to grind their batches'.

5 The soft sandstone rocks of the Hermitage are capped with a layer of conglomerate. The site of past dwellings and a chapel.

6 A large cave, several yards distance from the Hermitage caves, was brick faced with door and windows *c*.1900 for the use of the custodian. Mr. Cyril Taylor used the cave as a holiday home until the 1930s. Five generations of his family had lived there as custodians of the caves.

7 An 1848 view by Shropshire artist, John Cox Bayliss, depicts the cistern (between the churches) on Castle Hill. The first iron cistern, provided in 1707 by William Whitmore, stood in the garden of Governor's house where the brick base remains. It was soon moved and erected on a raised base on Castle Walk. It received water from the waterwheel in the Severn for 146 years. The houses on the left of the picture backed on to the old caves shown in Joseph Powell's drawings of 1830. Built in 1840, they were occupied until the 1970s.

8 The library on Castle Hill, was built *c.*1836 and catered for the leisured classes. The upper storey was removed in 1912. To its right is the Green which in the 18th century had faced on to the bowling green, now the Castle grounds. Below these buildings, off library steps, many old caves can be seen. The white house on the river side was the *George and Dragon*, a favourite haunt of the river men. Its wharf was most likely the King's Loade, where supplies were off-loaded for the castle.

9 A barge moored off the Bylet with a wherry carrying passengers downstream. Note the water cistern clearly showing on the skyline. By the early 19th century there was quite considerable passenger traffic. As late as 1844, there was a regular service three times a week from Shrewsbury to Gloucester. (Published in *Picturesque Views of Staffordshire and Shropshire*, 1830.)

10 A lithograph of the view of Bridgnorth from across the river by Mary Stringer in 1844. A local artist, she lived at 3 Church Street. George Bellett, author of *The Antiquities of Bridgnorth*, was the incumbent of St Leonard's at this time. He put through the long overdue restoration of the church in the early 1860s. Until then, the north aisle, destroyed during the Civil War, had not been replaced. Note the toll house and gate on New Road.

11 Bridge Street, soon after the new clock was provided in 1876. The clock tower was rebuilt in 1960 in order to widen the bridge. At that time the industrial building nearby was demolished. In an earlier improvement in 1824, the *Bull* (on the right) was partly demolished and rebuilt further back from the street. A six-bay dwelling house, the Lyon, stood on the site in 1612. The present building, now the rugby club, retains many old beams.

TREVITHICKS,
PORTABLE STEAM ENGINE,

Catch me who can.

Mechanical Power Subduing Animal Speed.

12 John Hazeldine, the foundry owner, was chosen by Trevithick to build several steam engines for agricultural and other uses in the early 19th century. One of these, built in 1808, was exhibited as a railway engine in London and, as visitors paid to have rides round the circuit, it can rightly claim to have been the first fare-paying passenger railroad.

13 The multi-armed signpost and ephemeral telephone kiosk on the junction between Mill Street and St John Street, *c.*1930. The manager of J.C. Lloyd, grocer appears in his doorway.

14 First recorded as an inn in 1840, it occupies two burgage plots. The house on the plot adjoining Doctors Lane was demolished *c*.1730. In 1720, the left-hand plot had been leased to a Bridgnorth glazier, a dwelling there having been recently pulled down. He, at his own cost, built a 'good, firm and substantial dwelling', some of which might be incorporated into the present early 19th-century building.

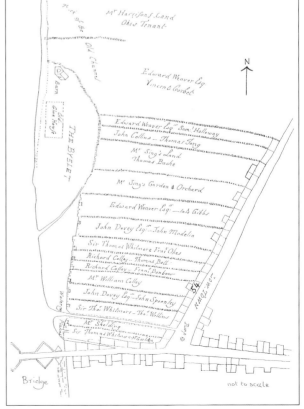

15 When the Bylet was conveyed in 1768 it was with the proviso that William Colley, living at no.54 'his heirs and assigns … will have the liberty to pass and repass at all times with horses and wagons from their messuage over the Gravelly Bylet to the river'. This house, and many others in Mill Street, were provided with malt houses when built in the early 18th century.

16 When auctioned in 1865 these cottages in Mill Street included three further dwellings (sharing one wash house) joined at right angles to the brick house on the left of the photograph. One of the three late 16th-century timber-framed cottages, no.43, was occupied for many years during the 19th century by William Jones, followed by his son Elisha, both coopers whose workplace was behind their premises. No.39, formerly the *Crown and Anchor*, in 1865 was also a butcher's shop.

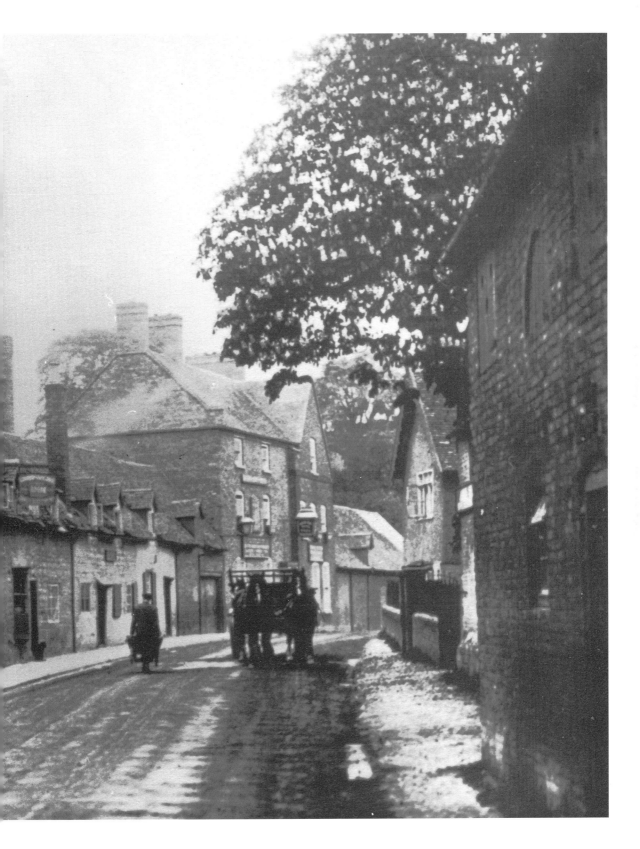

17 *Left.* Cann Hall, erected *c.*1360 and rebuilt in 1594, where Prince Rupert is reputed to have spent a night in 1642. He sent a note to the Jury for the election of new Bailiffs, exhorting its members to choose those well-affected to the King. In the mid-18th century it housed a factory making sulphuric acid by the 'new' cheaper lead chamber process. Its status declined during the 19th century. A stone mason occupied part of the premises, moving in soon after the cemetery was built nearby in 1856 and was still there when this photograph was taken *c.*1890. Cann Hall, demolished in 1960, gave its name to the bypass directly linking the Kidderminster and Wellington roads.

18 *Below left.* In the foreground is the *Rock Inn*, pre-1892. In the distance the water works had replaced the waterwheel in 1853, pumping up filtered water to the reservoir behind High Rock. This benefited, in particular, the people of Low Town who had, until then, to pump water from their wells. Spring water was not available there until the 1870s.

19 Built in 1811 in gothic style, Apley Park included the frontage of a sham private chapel hiding the corner of a previous Georgian house. William Whitmore bought the estate in 1582. His descendants bought property until, by the end of the 18th century, they owned 12,000 acres of Shropshire, the Castle (at the King's disposal during the Civil War) and the advowsons of six local churches. By this means the Whitmores had increased their influence in Bridgnorth to the extent that at least one of them was returned to Parliament at every election between the Restoration and 1870, only excepting 1710. On three occasions they occupied both Bridgnorth seats. Thus the saying grew up, 'all on one side like a Bridgnorth election'.

BURGESSES OF **BRIDGNORTH.**

BEWARE OF

The United Family Compact,

CONSISTING OF

The East India Company, The Bank of England, and all its Branches, with the Ministry, all united together to preserve their

◆UNJUST MONOPOLIES!◆

So injurious to a good Trade.

Be true to yourselves, and your best Friend,

W. WOLRYCHE

Whitmore, Esq.

AND VOTE FOR HIM.

GOD SAVE THE KING!

GITTON, PRINTER, BRIDGNORTH.

20 The outcome of the 1830 election aroused much interest in Calcutta. As this poster shows, Mr. Whitmore was opposed to the trading privileges of the East India Company!

21 *Right.* W. Wolryche Whitmore, a Whig, advocated changes to the Corn Laws. He supported consumers opposing high prices, which would have benefited farmers and landlords. To the chagrin of Bridgnorth Tories he had had, in previous elections, the support of Thomas Whitmore of Apley, a Tory M.P. Such antagonism to the family monopoly was aroused, as it had been on many earlier occasions, that Wolryche Whitmore decided to stand for election in Wolverhampton.

TO THE

Worthy & Independent

ELECTORS

OF

BRIDGNORTH.

GENTLEMEN,

Finding on my return into the County, that three Gentlemen have already appeared as Candidates for the Borough of Bridgnorth, at the next Election, and that an expectation of a declaration of my intentions very naturally prevails, I take this early opportunity of informing you, that under existing circumstances, it is not my intention to offer myself to your notice at the next Election.

I am induced to take this step, on account of the change which the Reform Bill has made in the Constituency of Bridgnorth;—giving a greatly increased weight to local Interests, and imparting to it a character of a more decidedly Agricultural description.

The former circumstance might not only have the effect of rendering my return to Parliament precarious, but also place some of my best Friends in the unpleasant predicament of being called upon to make a sacrifice, either of their feelings, or their interest.

The latter would probably operate with equal, or greater force against my re-Election; inasmuch as I am decidedly of opinion, that a considerable change in the Laws regulating the admission of Foreign Corn should take place;—a change which I fear the Agricultural Interest may still regard as injurious to their prospects: though calculated, in my judgment, to promote the real and permanent prosperity of all classes, including the Agricultural.

It is, Gentlemen, with great reluctance I have brought myself to this determination. I entertain, and shall ever continue to feel, a lively and a grateful sense of the warm and cordial support I have, for several years, met with from you; and I can assure you, that though Political connexion may have ceased between us, I shall ever regard the Borough of Bridgnorth with a most friendly Interest, and do all that lies in my power to promote the welfare of its Inhabitants.

I remain, Gentlemen,

Your much obliged, and obedient Servant,

W. W. WHITMORE.

Dudmaston, June 12, 1832.

GITTON, PRINTER, BRIDGNORTH.

June 14th 1832. —

300

MORFE
COURSING   MEETING.

ON THURSDAY & FRIDAY, the 23rd & 24th of JANUARY, 1834.

ALL AGED

CUP AND GOBLET.

1.	Mr. Hincksmans blk. d. Spectre,............against	Mr. Davenport's red d. Dragoon.
2.	Hon. R. Hill's blk. d. Heretic, ...——	Mr. Bache's fawn d. Baron.
3.	Mr. Bache's red b. Bracelet,............——	Mr. Hincksman's black & white d. Hero.
4.	Mr. Harris's red d. Hudibras,............——	Mr. H. Hill's blk. & white b. Hirundo.
5.	Mr. Vickers's red d. Victor,............——	Mr. Davenport's blk. b. Drill.
6.	Mr. Vickers's fawn b. Vanish, ...——	Mr. Bates's red d. Burgundy.

FIRST TYE.

Winner of No. 1. against the Winner of No. 2.
Winner of No. 3. against the Winner of No. 4.
Winner of No. 5. against the Winner of No. 6.

MORFE SWEEPSTAKES,

ONE SOVEREIGN EACH.

1.	Mr. H. Campbell's brin. b. Hornpipe,......against	Mr. H. Hill's red. b. Hora.
2.	Mr. Vickers's blk. d. Velocipede, ...——	Mr. Hincksman's white b. Venus.
3.	Mr. Davenport's red b Daisy, ...——	Mr. Vickers's blk. d. Vaulter.
4.	Mr. Bache's blue & white b. Butterfly,......——	Mr. Davenport's blk. b. Deborah.

FIRST TYE.

Winner of No. 1. against the Winner of No. 2.
Winner of No. 3. against the Winner of No. 4.

MATCHES.

1.	Mr. Bache's red d. Brutus,.........against	Mr. Hincksman's wh. b. Milliner.
2.	Mr. H. Campbell's b. Huguent, ...——	Mr. Bache's fawn b. Bellona.

GITTON AND SMITH, PRINTERS.

22 From the left, St John's House, Diamond Hall and the houses demolished the following year to make way for the Cann Hall bypass. Diamond Hall was built by Roger Pope, M.P. In 1685 he commemorated his racing win, on a horse called 'Diamond', with a weather vane showing horse and rider. Diamond Hall has survived while two houses on the St John's Hospital site have since been demolished. An archaeological excavation in 1977 revealed seven skeletons in its 13th- to 17th-century cemetery.

23 Coursing, one of the ancient British sports, became popular in the 19th century. Horse races held on Morfe, the earliest recorded in 1718, had ceased on the enclosure of the common in 1812.

24 Bridgnorth boats had a large part of the coal trade on the Severn, operating almost until the end of the 19th century. Coal was transported cheaply from Broseley. Michael Meredith, maltster and coal merchant, distributed coal from the wharf at the end of Doctors Lane. The row of cottages upstream had been built for Hazeldine foundry workers.

25 Southwell and Co., having their main factory on the west bank, by 1835 had built two small carpet factories over the river on Foundry Yard and had provided some housing for their workforce. By 1840 these factories had been taken over by Thomas Elcock, who continued carpet production. By 1856 he had replaced the buildings with two small malt houses shown in this early photograph *c.*1860. The family of Daniel Phillips was making clay tobacco pipes on Foundry Yard until the turn of the century. Further upstream, on the west bank is the toll keeper's cottage. The tolls, charged on the horses, financed the upkeep of the towpaths.

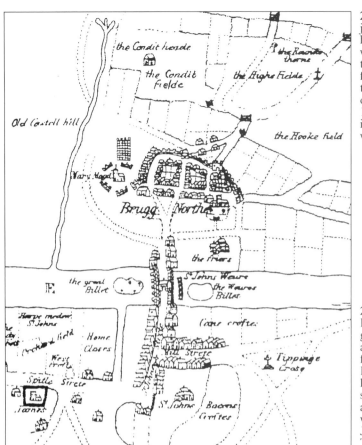

26 Detail of old map showing St John's weir just above the bridge, belonging then to the hospital in St John's Street. Fish nets and straps were suspended from timber frames built across the shallow part of the river. A channel was formed to the north and south of the bridge for the use of river traffic, thus causing the formation of the two bylets. The north bylet, when leased in 1587, was called the Neade Bylett or Gravell, indicating that the channel had silted up after the weir had been removed.

27 St Osyth's Chapel, conducted by the Grey Friars until the Dissolution, was housed in the gatehouse, probably in the room over the archway. From 1699 until the building of their first chapel in West Castle Street in 1704, Bridgnorth Baptists met in the gatehouse. The lean-to was the toll-keeper's cottage which survived the demolition of the gatehouse in 1801 and remained until the projecting timber struts were washed away in 1819. (An engraving by J. Walker from an original drawing by J.M.W. Turner, R.A., 1794.)

28 The bridge in 1939, little changed since 1823, when John Smallman of Quatford widened the centre by fitting flat ironwork at the sides of the stone arches. He replaced stone parapets with open ironwork, adding a touch of elegance. The bridge approach had been improved in 1852 when the old *Hop Pole Inn*, standing between the bridge and the harbour master's house (seen here bottom right), had been demolished. On the far bank, part of the track of the old channel of the north bylet is in evidence.

29 After a false start in 1879, bowling on the bylet was revived in 1886. A bridge replaced the ferry three years later. Note the coracle in the channel, used for eel fishing. By this date the river trade had almost finished.

30 Ridley's warehouse at the west end of the bridge, where water levels are recorded on the old wall. Between this wall and the recommencement of the towpath there was a small dock (partly blocked in this photograph of 1977) from which goods were hoisted into the warehouse.

31 A boat travelling upstream had to stop at the quay. Its horse was led to the far side of the bridge, through an entry from the Cartway back to the interrupted towpath. In the meantime, the head of the boat was drawn out to the second arch by means of a rope thrown over from the bridge. One end of the towrope, with a billet attached, was thrown from the north side of the bridge to float under the second arch to be fished out and attached to the lowered mast. The other end of this towrope was thrown from the bridge to be attached to the horse waiting near the small dock area. (This completed, the boat was able to continue upstream.)

32 The building on the left was a licensed lodging house in 1871. The warehouses belonged to the *Beehive* which fronted on to the Cartway. It housed 17 lodgers and a family of eight at that time. The carpet works chimney seen in Friar Street was removed in the 1980s. The large, three-storey house facing the bridge, once occupied by the gas works manager, was demolished when the carpet works expanded. (The gas works can be seen upstream.)

33 The steps, arched over and beneath the gate seen in plate 32, may have been used to put the bowhaulers ashore after being ferried home. The photograph dates from 1857.

34 Still recognisable in this 1857 photograph are 3-8 Riverside and 5 Bank Steps. The houses between have been demolished. In 1895, the collapse of a retaining wall on the rock behind killed two people, injured others and made 13 families homeless. The kitchens at the back of these houses had been hewn out of the rock and archways, still visible in the towpath wall, would have led to their cellars.

35 The road to the gas works under construction, carried out as 'relief work' for the unemployed poor during the severe winter of 1887. On the right of the picture the road is being raised above the towpath wall.

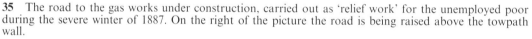

36 The construction of the raised towpath in front of the houses *c.*1800 enabled horses to replace gangs of men (bowhaulers). The iron band on top of the wall prevented wear on the rope. Some of the band still remains, bearing marks from the ropes.

37 Darley's and Corfield's, on opposite banks of the river, had hired out pleasure boats since the 1890s. At the time of this photograph, 1912, Corfield's were advertising the *Queen of the Severn*, a first-class party boat with a piano on board. G. Corfield of Severn Terrace also had boats for hire. The 1930 town carnival concluded with a river carnival in the evening.

38 Darley's boats, bungalow and tea garden in 1925, with the Wilson and Hood malthouse then in its last year of malt production. The single-storey extension, built in 1882, was the Bridgnorth Rowing Club boat house until the club disbanded in 1927.

39 Pictured *c*.1920, the men's coxed four with Walter Broster as cox. After a false start in 1864, the reformation of the Rowing Club was prompted in 1868 by a match held at Bridgnorth between Cheltenham College and Shrewsbury School when reportedly it 'presented an extensive scene of fashionable spectators never before equalled in Bridgnorth'.

40 Bridgnorth Regatta, 1964. Colin Lloyd winning the novice sculls. Until the First World War, regatta events included swimming, coracle racing and walking the pole (projecting over the river). The prize for the last was a couple of fat ducks! The floating swimming baths, first moored on the riverside in 1878, were later owned by the Rowing Club.

41 This timber-framed property beside Friars Steps (one room up, one down) was included in a survey of corporation property in 1693. Also included were six cave-houses facing the river, one of them 'newly erected'. A large percentage of the riverside population was employed in river work.

42 Bales of wool delivered to the carpet works by wagon after the construction of the road along Riverside (1887). Previously the only access for wheeled vehicles had been along Friar Street. By 1890 the works had been extended four times, five bays being added each time.

43 *Above right*. This photograph of 1875 shows the site of the water wheel (near the gable end of Ridley's warehouse) which had for 146 years forced water up to the reservoir tank on Castle Walk using only water power. Though built to rise and fall with the river level, on many occasions water rents had to be refunded due to low water level. A breach in the main pipe plus heavy rain had, in 1718, caused a landslide, bringing down a house 'which slided from off the rock', falling into the tan pits.

44 *Right*. The beauty of Bridgnorth attracted many famous artists at the end of the 18th century including Farington, Girtin, Powell, Turner, O'Neil and Sandby, whose picture here of the water wheel and bridge is dated 1770. Artistic licence accentuates the height of the wheel from the water and replaces the warehouses with cottages. The bridge-end warehouse is also depicted as a more exuberant building.

45 Mr. Dick Brown's ferry boat in Underhill Street in 1946. The river had always been subject to flooding, and floods in 1947 followed the worst snow blizzards in living memory with a gale that reached 90 miles an hour. At least a hundred houses were affected and the mayor opened a fund for victims.

46 Despite all traffic being diverted up and down Cartway in the floods of 1960, this petrol tanker still attempted to reach the beleaguered garage! Families living nearby in George and Dragon Yard and also those in Severn Terrace were forced to evacuate their homes. An emergency rest centre was set up at the Castle Hall, but all those evacuated found temporary accommodation with friends or relations.

47 The site of the chief boat-building yard, next to William Oakes' house. A large number of trows, barges and wherries had been built here for the river trade before the yard closed in 1868. Some sea-going vessels had also been constructed. One, launched in 1850, described in the *Wolverhampton Chronicle* as 96 ft. overall length to carry 250 tons, was built for use in the Baltic-Gloucester timber trade.

48 Bate's timber yard at 40 Underhill Street, *c*.1890. In the centre is Mr. Horne, who later became part of the building firm Horne and Meredith.

49 The carpenters at Bate's building yard. From 1885 to 1900 William Bate had premises at 66 Whitburn Street and workshops at 40 Underhill Street. The Underhill premises from 1900 to 1950 were occupied by T.E. Lay, builders and contractors.

50 Underhill Street runs along between the cliff and the Severn. The 1861 census listed malthouses, stables, warehouses, iron moulders and blacksmiths, all making use of the caves behind. Near the bottom of Library steps was Lay's Coach and Paint Shop, here with Messrs. Roberts, Hammond and C. Lewis in the doorway. Before demolition in the 1960s these premises were used by Micrometric Engineering.

51 At the other end of Underhill Street (no. 44 Cartway) Roden's Foundry, pictured in 1908, was in business from the 1860s until *c*.1926, advertised as Engineer, Millwright and Smith, Iron and Brass Founder. These premises were later used by Bridgnorth Engineering.

52 Bishop Percy's house, so called after Thomas Percy, born there in 1729, had been built by Richard Forster in 1580. It was used as an iron foundry by the Barker family *c*.1850-70. Separated from the *Red Lion* by steps, it had a footpath leading to the river. Note the wagon slippers in the doorway.

53 Bishop Percy's house restored. A 1952 advert for Magpie House quoted a local historian: 'In the north wall of one of the bedrooms was a wooden shutter—used on Sunday mornings to pass beer through to lodgers in Jones' tramps lodging house!' In 1871 James Foxall occupied the Magpie, while next door was Benjamin Jones, waterman and lodging house keeper.

54 Bank Steps, leading from opposite the white-fronted house in Cartway to the lamp post below, was another route from the riverside up to High Town. Above left is the United Reformed and Methodist Chapel, built 1843, pictured from the rear, which also fronts on to Cartway.

55 Stoneway Steps from the *Album of Bridgnorth Views*, *c*.1894. The longest and most dramatic of the steps are cut deep into the rock. Wall braces known locally as 'Pope's Spectacles', after the Low Town foundry that made them, were installed in the 19th century.

56 The river trade was at its height in the early 18th century when the *Black Boy* was built on the steep Cartway (then the main route for horse-drawn vehicles between High Town and Low Town). Stout bars across the windows were necessary when the frontage was altered in the 19th century. This part of the town was notorious for riotous and bawdy behaviour! The 1851 census shows six lodging houses and five inns housing 89 Irish folk, the men walking daily to and from the farms where they laboured. Later, many of the railway 'navvies' found lodging here. John Cole, Chief Constable, in his 'Journal 1860-67' describes a 'nightmare time' on Saturday nights when mobs congregated brawling and fighting. 'With only one other constable', he wrote, 'it was dangerous to try and keep the peace.' The area's reputation lingered on well into the 20th century.

57 The house on the right, at the junction of Cartway and Friar Street, had been kept by the Orchard family as a beer house in 1855. Then, in 1860, licensed as the *Railway Tavern*, it remained in the family until 1916. It was so named because it was frequented by the navvies employed in the construction of the railway tunnel which ran underneath the whole of High Town. Many of them lodged in Cartway. The two adjoining houses were demolished in the 1960s.

58 Mr. and Mrs. Joe Griffiths outside their home of Friar Street (now demolished). They emigrated to America in the early 1900s.

59 This view, painted by Joseph Farington in 1789 shows the recently opened New Road, the water reservoir on Castle Hill, the gatehouse on the bridge, Diamond Hall, St Leonard's Church on the highest point of the town and St Mary Magdalene Church behind the ruins of the castle.

60 This view from the Bull Ring Meadow *c*.1900 shows the town's first infirmary, built in 1836 (the three-storeyed building). It became St Joseph's Convent in 1896. A nun can be seen on the steps. The 'Tainter' wall, built in 1821 on the footing of the town walls, bounded an earlier tenter yard where woollen cloth was dried and stretched between tenterhooks. The cloth was produced on the site of St Leonard's School until 1760. The mouth of the railway tunnel can be seen on the right, where the cutting had destroyed part of the vineyard belonging to Bridgen Hall, seen here on the site of the present library car park.

61 View from the Cleobury Road *c*.1880. The cannon can be seen between the two elm trees where it was placed in 1858. From there a steep descent by Cannon Steps leads to the toll house on New Road, where tolls were collected until 1852. The New Road was improved and a footpath made in 1876 (a likely date for the demolition of the toll house). The timber yard on the right was reputedly the site of an earlier boat-building yard. Behind are the houses of George and Dragon Yard.

62 A photograph taken before the building of the first footbridge in 1894. St Leonard's School is seen as it was rebuilt in 1855, before its enlargement at the turn of the century. The Folly Hole, a steep sandstone gully running from Holly Bush Road to the top of New Road, was most likely the old route up from King's Loade to the castle.

63 On 31 January 1862, a public holiday in Bridgnorth, a special train left Worcester. Seven carriages were reserved for directors and guests, each provided with a small hamper and bottle of wine. The band of the Bridgnorth Volunteer Rifle Brigade rode in a special coach, dismounting to play the train's arrival into Bridgnorth station. Before the train continued to Shrewsbury the mayor, Mr. W. Jones, entertained the V.I.P.s at a drinks party. On their return from Shrewsbury, the V.I.P.s were escorted through crowded streets to a reception and public banquet in the New Assembly Rooms (New Market Building). Bridgnorth Council honoured the occasion further by granting approximately 650 'deserving poor' 2 oz. of tea, loaves of bread and up to 1 cwt. of coal per household. On the extreme right is G. Dukes.

64 The railway footbridge was opened in 1895, thus providing a much easier access for foot passengers between the High Town and the station. This photograph gives a splendid view of Panpudding Hill which gave besiegers of the castle down the years such a good position for cannon and other siege weapons. Its origins still give historians much to debate.

65 Cast in 1826 and decorated with the Czarist crest, this Russian gun was captured at the siege of Sebastopol in 1855. Public subscription paid for its transportation and erection on the southern tip of the castle grounds in 1858. It remained there until 1940 when a national appeal for scrap metal led to its final demise. The two elms were also taken down.

66 Bridgnorth Cycling Club, established in 1880, taken by T.C. Bromwich in 1885 in the castle grounds. The club's officials included a road captain, his deputy and a bugler. Club runs were held on Thursday evenings during the season. On a visit to the Danery in 1885, they rode single file, bicyclists leading and tricyclists following. For the return journey, assembly was sounded by the bugler. A bugle had been won at the Shrewsbury Horticultural Fête in 1883 and in 1885 the club was awarded a silver-plated bugle for having the largest muster at the Shropshire and West Midlands Meet of Cyclists. It is now on display in the Bridgnorth museum.

67 To mark the Diamond Jubilee of Queen Victoria in 1897, Mr. W.O. Foster of Apley made over to the town the Old Tower Field, to be laid out as a pleasure garden. Later that year Mrs. W.O. Foster opened the completed grounds and planted an oak tree in the north-west corner. Messrs. H. and M. Southwell (carpet manufacturers) erected a handsome bandstand in the grounds. Seen here are, from left to right, standing: Hazelwood, R. Findon, J. Cooper (Cooper and Woolley), F. Nock, Dr. Bethel, F. Callant (with spade), Bennett (gas manager), Mr. Barnes (surgeon), Rev. Dillon, C. MacMichael, R. Nicholas, Morell, C. Turnbull, Taylor (solicitor), Mayor Edmund Southwell, Rev. Parsons, Hazelwood (Castle hill), Martin Southwell, F. Cooksey, J.H. Cooksey (town clerk), Major Westcott, W. Southwell, G. Stewart, W.O. Foster, B. Deighton, Anderson, Nichols, Haines, Archdeacon Oldham, Dr. Rhodes, Rev. Knight, Rev. Gledhill, Merrick, Kirby-Minton, C.H. Cunnington (headmaster, Blue Coats School), Trevor, P.C. Lowe; seated: Mr. Wyley, Mr. Burton, Mrs. E. Southwell, Mrs. W.O. Foster and Miss Evelyn Foster.

58 The landscaping of the Old Tower Field provided an 'ornamented pleasure ground' marking Victoria's Diamond Jubilee. In 1876 a rounded apse, designed by Blomfield, had been added to St Mary's Church.

59 These new gates to the Castle Grounds, erected in 1957 by public subscription, to the memory of former Mayor Roly Bowen, were opened by the Duchess of Kent. Outside the grounds can be seen the drinking fountain surmounted by the bronze figure of Sabrina, the Roman name for the river Severn, and decorated with the borough seal. Erected in 1881, in memory of Henry Whitmore of Apley M.P., it has since been moved into the Castle Grounds.

70 The Catholic Apostolic Church in West Castle Street, built in 1850. The *Bagshaw Directory* quoted: 'The congregation is under the rule and government of the apostles, being in the charge of an angel who, with priests assisted by deacons, fulfil their several duties clothed in appropriate vestments'. The building was bought in 1950 by the town council. Major alterations were made in 1970 when the front wall was removed and a brick frontage built to enclose the old east window.

71 A warehouse used by Thomas Deighton, maltster, photographed *c*.1860. The adjoining property, 2 West Castle Street, was then the post office. Charles MacMichael, postmaster, was also a currier. The yard behind the properties had a leather drying house and an engine house. The remnants of a tan yard which had occupied part of the site were acquired for the New Market Buildings.

72 By 1896 the warehouse had been converted into the post office.

73 The post office, shortly after it opened in 1902. Charles Deighton, wine and spirit merchant at 30/31 High Street by the 1880s, had retained some of the Deighton malthouse property of the 1860s. The Branch Trunk Line of the National Telephone Company had been extended to Bridgnorth in 1898.

74 Postern gate, *c.*1875. On the right is the entrance to the timber-framed building 7/8 Waterloo Terrace. This was the *Talbot Inn* from the 17th century until the late 18th century. William Smith's Plan of 1820 indicates that its stabling had been on part of the site of the New Market Buildings.

75 Plan of New Market Buildings, equipped and ready in 1861. The local Board of Health, in conjunction with the Bridgnorth Public Buildings and Market Company Ltd., opened the building with the intention of clearing the traders, stalls and produce from the High Street, but only one stallholder moved in. After storms of protest from the townspeople the market was allowed to continue in the street on condition that the stalls were not sublet. In a celebrated court case, 10 of the stallholders won on the grounds that there could be no interference with the prescriptive rights of stallage in the street.

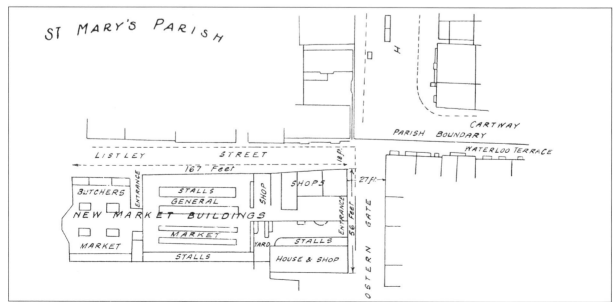

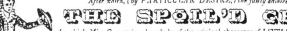

76 Theatre bill of 1828. The New Theatre, at Postern Gate, built in 1824 by John Smallman of Quatford for the Corporation, was very popular.

77 Top station of the Castle Hill Railway, photographed *c*.1895. The cars were originally operated hydraulically, water being pumped into a tank on the top of the car at the top station until it was heavy enough to raise the lower car. When the car with the full tank reached the bottom station, the water was pumped out and the tank on the top car was filled. This method was continued until 1944 when the water pumps were abandoned in favour of electrical winding gear. Note the iron gates—these were erected at each end of Castle Walk to stop animals straying on fair days.

78 Castle Terrace is an ancient passage leading to the castle precincts. The one-roomed cottage (dated 1665), next to the 19th-century house on the left, is joined by two earlier timber-framed cottages. The end cottage near the steps is the side of the 17th-century property at 1 Waterloo Terrace, its basement is a shop on Castle Terrace. The steps lead up to Waterloo Terrace, raised above the Cartway on which, facing the camera, can be seen no.97. Today, with mock timber framing removed, it houses a shop 'Natural Things'!

79 3 Castle Terrace, *c*.1900. Now a private house, this small building between the Stoneway Steps and Castle Terrace served as a confectioner's from 1903 until the early 1960s.

80 Staff of the three shops of W. Jones and Co., 1896: Waterloo House (draper and silk merchant), 6 Waterloo Terrace (hardware dealer, sewing machine and cycle agent) and 57 High Street (chinaware). This photograph was taken at the rear of Waterloo House. The shed behind, approached over wooden planks, was stocked with canvas and thrums (woollen offcuts for the carpet works). Many orders for these were received from overseas and from the Royal Navy.

81 There was plenty of choice here for the keen cyclist at the turn of the century. It was usual to display as many goods as possible on the pavement. Here on Waterloo Terrace the shopkeepers pose with a wide assortment of goods including a mangle and a firegrate.

82 Amos Ryder opened this clothier's shop at 7 Waterloo Terrace in the early 1890s. He had previously been in partnership with Ryder and Scott, linen and wool drapers, who had moved into 65 High Street in 1875, when Corser's moved to their present premises. 'Friendly House' later became 'Ryder's Toy Bazaar'.

83 Waterloo Terrace, dated by the cars *c.*1967. 'Friendly House' had become Ryder's Toy Bazaar and later Ryder's Cash Store. It closed in 1970.

84 Cooper, Purton and Sons, founded in 1810, moved into their new building on this site in 1828. As agents for the Bank of England they issued Bank of England notes. They also used Bridgnorth bank notes, issued by the London bankers Williams, Deacon and Labouchere, featuring a view of the town from the south east. Taken over in 1889 by the Metropolitan and Birmingham Banking Company they, in turn, were replaced by the London and Midland Bank who occupied this building in the early days of motoring, 1914-23.

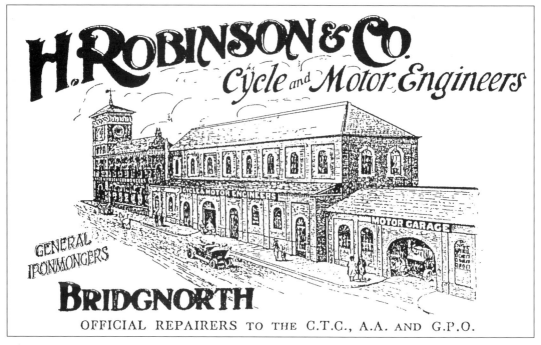

85 Another change of use for New Market Buildings came in 1911 when the Wolverhampton firm of H. Robinson and Co. moved in to the existing ironmonger's premises and took up the whole of the ground floor of the building to cater for the rapidly increasing cycle and motor business.

86 J.W. Lester was a butcher's shop in Listley Street until the First World War. After the war it became, briefly, the Unemployment Office, but then returned to retail use, first as a general store, then later as a tobacconist and confectioner. Today it is run by the Southall family and retains its period charm by selling a range of home-made sweets and locally made walking sticks.

87 Top of Railway Street in 1939. The site of the small Listley Gate in the old town wall.

88 *Woodman Inn*, outing to Church Stretton in 1923. Left to right: (top row) W. Breakwell, Ern Bills; (middle row) Ben Perry, Jack Beddoes, J. Chaplin, Joe Edwards, Harry Cook, W. Oakley, Jack Jennings; (bottom row) Jack Hadley, Fred Lloyd, Charlie Speke, Ern Speke, Bob Callant and son Les; driver: George Jones Junior.

89 The Blakemore family kept the *Bricklayers Arms* in Listley Street 1880-1920. It was demolished in 1958 to make way for the Comrades Club. The side door led to a Smithfield which was licensed by Clement Edkins in 1867 and used until the opening of Nock Deighton's Smithfield behind Whitburn Street in 1907. On fair days the streets were used. Listley Street in 1881 was described as 'literally crammed with young Cheshire and Irish cattle'.

90 The *Robin Hood*, 6 Listley Street, *c.*1900. In use as a tavern from the 18th century, it was demolished in 1968 to make a back entrance to Tesco in the High Street.

91 The Cavalier café in 1938 was above Tyler's, men's outfitters at 45 High Street. In the 1940s Tyler's replaced these adjoining offices with an extension in line with the other buildings. This later became the Ladies Shop.

92 The early hostelry, the *Pig and Castle*, later the *Castle*, was an important posting house and coaching inn in the early 19th century. From the 1860s the property was used half as an inn and half as linen drapers. Thomas Whitefoot, proprietor of the *Crown*, set up the 'Castle Wine Stores' here in 1875, restoring the building and exposing the timber framing. The four wooden carved figures, which had formerly decorated the gallery which stretched along the back of the hostelry, were placed in their present position between the bays on the frontage. In 1925 Thomas Whitefoot retired and sold the two-generation business to Tanners, wine merchants of Shrewsbury.

93 The carved wooden figures now adorning the frontage of Tanners wine merchants appear to represent a woman holding a skull, the bust of a philosopher on a pedestal, a courtesan holding an hour glass and a lute player who has fallen asleep.

94 42 High Street was occupied by John Rogers, watchmaker at the end of the 18th century, became a private residence and then was inhabited, in succession, by two surgeons. Josiah Steward, MPS, PhC, set up his business in 1854. The pharmacy continued here, over four generations, until the early 1980s when the property became 'George and Bertie's', a bakery and café, retaining the decorative sign and frontage.

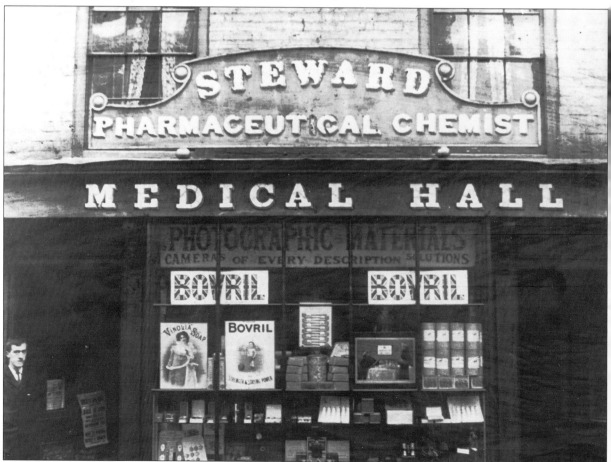

95 George Webb, lace dealer, traded here throughout the 1860s, selling Nottingham lace and also, no doubt, some of the traditional hand-made lace made by the local women. The Webb family continued here as linen drapers. The last member of the family, Miss Nellie Webb who sold baby linen and millinery, gave up in the 1940s. The sign came down, but the shop front was retained when Tesco's supermarket took over in 1969. The frontage still remains as the shop windows of W.H. Smith.

96 The entrance archway under the mid-18th-century building formerly the site of the *Cock and Castle* inn, leads to *The Court* a quiet, elegant cul-de-sac just off the High Street (named *The Square* on old maps).

97 A private mansion was recorded here in 1392 and when, in 1444, the family owners acquired the swan crest of the Bohun family by marriage, the mansion also acquired the name. In 1492 it was recorded as a hospice Le Swanne. Remnants of the piazzas described in the introduction can be seen along the frontage. Partly rebuilt after the Civil War, it was first officially licensed in 1690, but has never been a coaching inn due to lack of access for stabling. Mr. Mudd's shop, seen here 1875-6, continued as a fishmonger's right up to 1994 when, as Crane's, it closed and is now a curtaining shop. Next door can be seen the 'Bell Vaults', with its large bell.

98 The passage between Mudd's shop and the *Bell*, c.1870. This would have led earlier to the lane which joined Cartway and St Leonard's Church. The houses on the left have recently been restored with the help of English Heritage.

99 In 1887 Victoria's Golden Jubilee was celebrated over three days. All Sunday and day school children assembled wearing Jubilee medals and marched to a flower service at St Mary's Church.

100 The Diamond Jubilee parade in 1897 was an even grander affair than 10 years previously, medals were again struck, beacons lit and numerous events held both in High Town and on the river. Here the procession is led by Mayor Edmund Southwell, a partner with his father and brothers in H. and M. Southwell's Ltd., carpet manufacturers.

101 Medal struck to commemorate Queen Victoria's Diamond Jubilee.

102 Elephants escorted through the town *c.*1930 from the Innage recreation ground to bathe in the river.

103   There was no restriction on parking in the late 1920s and it was still usual to see droves of animals on their way to the Smithfield. The model T Ford is outside Miss Nellie Webb's millinery shop.

104   The Cycling Club celebrations at the turn of the century. Those present include: Fowles (tailor), Glaze, Ben Groves, Gough, Hawkins (plus dog), William Jones (Waterloo House), Morran, Palmer, Perkins and Callant (Waterloo Terrace), Speke, C. Brawn (fishmonger), C. Deighton, Edmonds, Richard Fendon (43 High Street, 1889-1903), C.H. Cunnington (Blue Coat School), J. Weaver (Whitburn Street shop), W. Williams (High Street shop), C. Tomkins and B. Tarrant (Waterloo House), Edmund Southwell (President), Mrs. Kyte, Mrs. Callant, Mrs. Cunnington.

105 A jack-in-the-box leads the procession of class 10 entries in this carnival, *c*.1910.

106 Civic Sunday parade, early 20th century. Firemen following the 'F' Company band. The mayor is in the horse-drawn carriage with mace bearers walking beside.

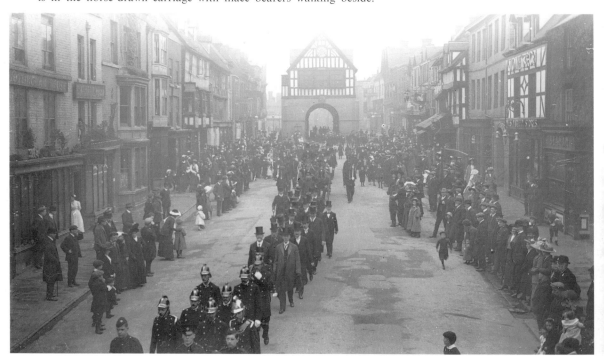

107 The High Street in 1863 before the building which became the Foster Memorial Institute was erected. Plaster covers the timber framing of the Town Hall bell tower and also the frontages of no.36 (the *Castle*) and the two adjoining properties. No.39, occupied by the doctors Thursfield from 1828-1909, had bay windows on the ground floor only (see below).

108 A recruiting drive in the High Street in 1875 with the battery of soldiers proceeding under and round the Town Hall. Note Dr. Thursfield's house, no.39 has added a bay window on the first floor and the timber framing on the *Castle* has been exposed.

109 The High Street in 1889 on the completion of the restoration of the Town Hall in commemoration of Victoria's Golden Jubilee. Gadsby, with the little dustpan as its emblem, had recently replaced Bromwich's shop. The *Bell Inn* sign can be seen opposite.

110 A conduit brought pure spring water to this place in the High Street near the old Butter Cross from medieval times. When the present Town Hall was built a fountain was incorporated in the southern end of the building. The Victorians built an underground reservoir to collect the water at this point. All along the pipe system, which brought the water down from Conduit Field in Oldbury, there were free standpipes and taps for public use.

111 George Case was a confectioner and baker at 68 St Mary's Street from 1890 to 1910.

112 Leonard Allen, mounted on Toby, *c.*1900, outside the entry leading to his grandmother's house behind 65 St Mary's Street. The newsagents, then kept by Thomas Oakley (see plate 113), became Allen's butcher's shop in 1903.

113 Thomas Oakley and his wife moved their newsagents from no.70 to no.65 St Mary's Street in 1900. Thomas, in the 1890s, was captain of Bridgnorth Town Football Club (see plate 114).

114 A late 1890s team of Bridgnorth Town Football Club (formed 1894-5) on the Innage Lane playing fields (now part of the infants' school). Thomas Oakley is seated centre (see plate 113). The team's strip was scarlet and black.

115 'F' (Bridgnorth) Company, King's Own Shropshire Light Infantry, Lieutenants G.C. Cooper and W. Westcott with prizewinners of the County Challenge Trophy 1898 outside the Drill Hall, St Mary's Street.

116 Colour Sergeants, past and present, of 'F' (Bridgnorth) Company, 1st Volunteer Battalion KSLI in 1900. Standing: Sgt. G. Lloyd, Sgt. J. Brown, Sgt. J. Moredike and Sgt. Instructor J. Harris. Seated: Sgt. C.H. Cunnington, Sgt. W. Westcott and Colour Sgt. H.T. Palmer. William Westcott was granted the honorary rank of major in 1903 and served until 1909. He was employed at the carpet factory, becoming a director of the company. C.H. Cunnington was headmaster of the Blue Coat School.

117 *Left.* Captain W.H. Westcott and Shooting Team 'F' Company (Bridgnorth), 4th Battalion KSLI (Territorial Force) Headquarters at the Drill Hall 1909-14. Front rank on the left is Lance Corporal F.A. Head, wearing above his right-hand pocket the T.F. Imperial Service Bar awarded to volunteers for overseas service prior to 1914.

118 *Bottom left.* Two medieval houses in St Mary's Street, possibly 15th-century. They were originally dwellings of one bay, single storey with croglofft (sleeping platform) at one end. No.46 still has post and truss construction open to view.

119 These evening lectures were a popular forerunner of the Mechanics' Institute formed in 1846 and Bridgnorth Literary and Scientific Institute formed in 1856.

THIS EVENING.
MR. MILLAR,
FROM LONDON,

Respectfully announces that he purposes delivering a Series of **Three Lectures** on the Principles and Operations of

Including Experiments in

ELECTRICITY, GALVANISM,
And Electro-Magnetism,

On Wednesday Evening, the 26th of February, 1840; and on Monday and Tuesday Evenings next, March the 2nd & 3rd. at Seven o'Clock,

IN THE TOWN HALL, BRIDGNORTH.

In the course of the Lectures the

CELEBRATED LAUGHING GAS

Will be introduced, and also a

BALLOON

With an ascending power of TEN STONE.

Tickets of admission to all the Lectures, only One Shilling; single night the same.

Abridged from the Birmingham Times.

"Mr. Millar concluded his course of Experimental Lectures last night, to one of the most numerous audiences we ever recollect to have seen assembled on a similar occasion. Three nights for a shilling was something new, and never was shilling better spent. We were glad to see so many ladies and young persons present. The experiments went off with great eclat. The Laughing Gas in particular excited much merriment, from the singular effects it produced on many individuals. One of the gravest old gentlemen in the room, and seemingly the most infirm, stepped forward and applied for the apparatus. Before he had inhaled the Gas half-a-minute he suddenly withdrew it, and with his finger and thumb fixed upon his nose, darted about the room with a velocity truly amazing ; to the great diversion of all, and the uproarious delight of the juveniles.

"We were astounded at the immense power of so small a Balloon. It carried up goodly sized persons with great rapidity. Many persons had an opportunity of ascending in a Balloon who never expected it. Wherever Mr. Millar goes he deserves crowded houses, for lowering his charges so much below the usual standard."

Tickets to be had at the Door.

Edkins and Son. Printers, Bridgnorth.

120 A battery of regular army Royal Horse Artillery in the High Street in 1875, probably on a recruiting drive. They would be billeted overnight in local inns. Two Senior N.C.O.s are wearing campaign medals, possibly won in the Crimean War or the Indian Mutiny. Note the clock on the Town Hall; in 1867 it was one of the first to be illuminated by gas.

121 In 1911, about the date of this photograph, an advertisement in the *Bridgnorth Almanac* stated that the *Cross Keys* was established in 1646. Harsh laws against Roman Catholics had been repealed in 1829 and in 1848 the shop and parlour were made into the first Roman Catholic chapel since the Reformation. From that time until it closed in the 1930s the licensed premises were at the rear of the building together with a cockfighting pit which attracted events with large prize money. This entry is now part of Barclays Bank building.

122 High Street, *c.*1875. Thomas Nock, founder of Nock Deighton's, had offices in the building adjoining the chemist (it later became the Foster Memorial Institute) and used the premises next door as a warehouse. The building with the imposing columns was the Worcester City and County Bank, built in 1855. In 1878 it became the Town Clerk's Office. The shop adjoining was Perry and Phillips, upholsterers and cabinet makers. In the building with the sunblind, Alderman Edkins printed and published the *Bridgnorth Journal.*

123 This long list of patent medicines was included in the four-page advertising leaflet of 1855.

124 In 1870 Bridgnorth's Town Clerk, Hubert Smith, travelled to Norway with gypsies who he had allowed to camp on his land and befriended. Over four years of travelling, a romance developed between him and the young Esmeralda. In 1874 they were married and returned to his house, 'The Mundens' in Bridgnorth. She refused to adapt to his way of life, preferring to sleep in the garden and in 1875, only six months after their return, she ran away with a young scholar Francis Groome. After her divorce from Hubert, she married Francis, but remained an intermittent wanderer until they finally parted in 1898. She lived on, occasionally visiting Bridgnorth, until her death in 1939.

25 Lloyd's shoe shop at 26 High Street. Note the beasts' heads on the frontage of Corser's next door.

26 Corser's were at 65 High Street in 1856. They built the present shop, no.25, in 1873. The Manchester House sign, here photographed c.1890, has gone, but the beasts still look down with blue eyes and ruby tongues.

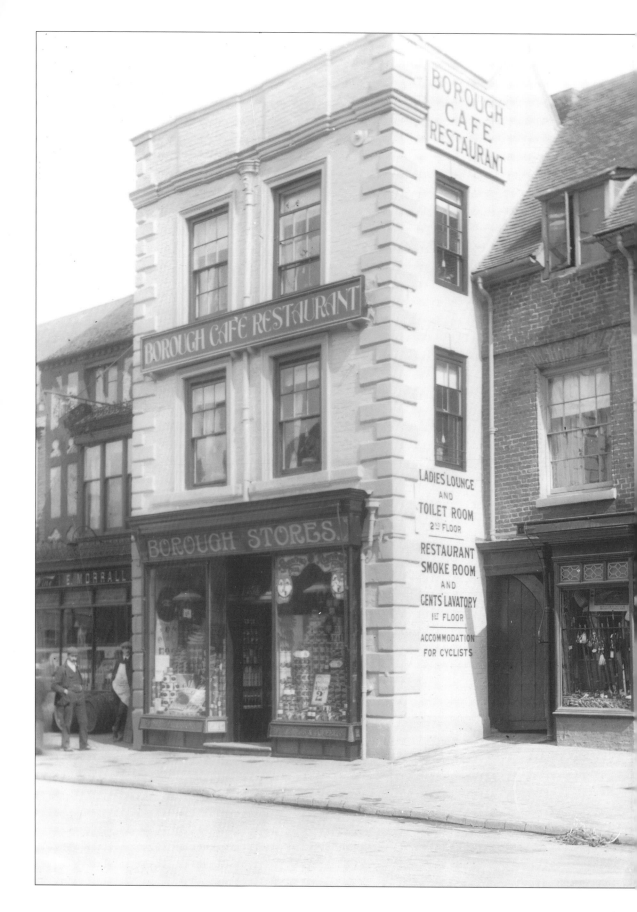

127 *Left.* This early 18th-century building, the Borough Café, shown here in 1908, was soon afterwards damaged by fire. It then became the Bridgnorth Garage. Next door Williamson and Sons, gunsmiths, gave up their business the following year. It was the end of an old Bridgnorth industry. In 1683, 20 locally-made muskets were seized from Bridgnorth inhabitants plotting against King Charles II in support of the Duke of Monmouth. Williamson's had moved from Birmingham to Waterloo Terrace *c.*1850.

128 'Arms they have none' proclaimed the Heralds on their visit to Bridgnorth in 1623. There were two seals of the Borough, one of which was lost in the Civil War. The matrix of the other, the Seal of Office of the Bailiffs, after having been mislaid over the years was discovered among scrap in the 1850s. Rev. Bellett, after taking an impression, deposited it in the British Museum. It was adopted by the Corporation as the 'Borough Arms', Rev. Bellet producing the motto 'In the Town's loyalty lies the King's safety'. It has been displayed on the Town Hall since 1875.

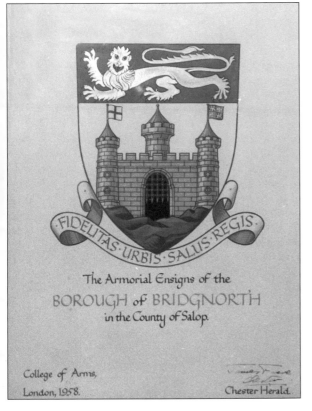

129 The Borough Seal, not having been registered with the College of Arms, was not a Coat of Arms. As part of the 800th Anniversary Charter Celebrations, the Arms were drawn up and registered in 1958. Rev. Bellet's motto, not technically part of the Arms, remains usable with them.

130 During the celebrations in 1957 of the 800th Anniversary of the granting of the town's first Royal Charter the Duchess of Kent, accompanied by the mayor, Charlie Hathaway, proceeded along the High Street to a dais in front of the *Crown Hotel*, where a guard of honour had been mounted by the Regimental Depot KSLI and RAF Bridgnorth.

131 Celebrations of the 800th Anniversary of the Royal Charter included street parties and maypole dancing. Among the maypole dancers here in the High Street are Kay Oliver and Jackie Wynne.

132 Lining up under the Town Hall for the Civic Sunday Parade in 1976 are: Len Morris (Town Marshal 1960-83), Special Sergeant McSorley and Special Constable Stuart (Mace Bearers), Douglas Wright (Town Clerk), Councillor Joe Chetter (Mayor), Councillor Jeff Walker (past Mayor), Councillor and Mrs. J. Simpson (Mayor and Mayoress of Much Wenlock), Councillor Bill Parr. The duty of Mace Bearer has since been taken over by Freemen of Bridgnorth.

133 1968—the second year of the sponsored Bridgnorth Walk. 409 seniors entered to walk 22 miles to the summit of the Brown Clee, returning to Severn Park. 80 juniors were taken by coach to Ditton Priors from where they walked to the summit and back. Their trophies were presented by a United States Lieutenant, then based at the Ditton Priors Depot. A 'Sorefoot Social' was held that evening in the Castle Hall. Later £1,860 was distributed to charities at Bishop Percy's House. Still an annual event, by 1994 the walk had to be limited to a thousand entries and the total money sponsored was £44,000.

134 Richard Baxter is reputed to have lived in this timber-framed house in St Leonard's churchyard when assistant minister 1639-41. A great performer and preacher, he became well-known for his Puritan views. Returning to preach after the Civil War he prayed that 'as the flames of war have consumed your houses, so may the Spirit of God consume the sin that was the cause'. Having called the people ignorant and dead hearted, he nevertheless dedicated his most famous book to 'my dearly beloved friends, the inhabitants of Bridgnorth'. Driven out of the Church in 1662, he was later tried by Judge Jeffries and imprisoned for sedition. This photograph dates from *c*.1890.

135 This fireman's house, photographed in *c*.1900, adjoined Richard Baxter's house in St Leonard's Close.

136 Mrs. Newsome in the doorway of Palmer's Hospital, *c.*1880. It was rebuilt in 1889. Almshouses for 10 poor widows were erected in St Leonard's churchyard in 1697 in memory of Colonel Billingsley by his nephew Francis Palmer. Colonel Billingsley, Commander of the Town Regiment, had been slain there on 31 March 1646, when Parliamentary infantry gained access by crossing rough ground from Love Lane, forcing their way across the deep, dry moat and through the palisade. A note written the following day by Stephen Tolly, Town Clerk and pinned into the Great Leet Book, described the day's action in Latin and ended 'The mind shudders to have mentioned it, and seeks refuge in tears'.

137 *Left*. The Girls' Public High School boarding house in St Leonard's Close was the home of the headmistress Miss Margaret Anderson. The dining room, pictured here in 1913, is now the Mayor's Parlour, College House. The girls' school, established in 1887, had from 1909 shared the new Grammar School building.

138 *Below left*. The cookery room of the Girls' High School in 1913. Cookery lessons continued in this room into the 1940s, remembered too as the break-time source of Horace Breakwell's penny buns. The Girls' High School later joined with the Boys' to form Bridgnorth Grammar School.

139 Dr. Rowley's pupils and the headmaster's house, St Leonards Close, by P. Browne, *c.*1860. The school, established in the 16th century, was at a very low ebb in 1821 when Thomas Rowley of Middleton Scriven was appointed headmaster. He was aged 24, a former pupil of Samuel Butler at Shrewsbury and an Oxford graduate. His success brought fame to the school, attracting boarders, who were accommodated in the headmaster's house and instructed in the 'Old Grammar School' on the opposite side of the Close. Dr. Rowley's terms in 1840 were: Entrance 3 guineas, Board and Tuition 40 guineas, Writing Master 3 guineas, Washing 3 guineas, Drawing, French and Dancing on the usual terms!

140 Land behind Town End, later called Salop Street, was still used for agriculture in the early 1870s. In 1878 a sale by auction of Fat and Store stock was held in the Smithfield behind the *Ash Inn*. The barns on the left were replaced by the houses of Albion Terrace in 1879. On the right of the picture was Thomas Porter's wheelwright's shop. The basement of the house adjoining the *Ash Inn* was where blind Archie Deans wove his baskets until 1974. Constable Cole manages to get into the picture.

141 The *Ash Inn*, shown here *c*.1880, outside the town walls on the road to Shrewsbury, had started its life as a farmhouse which was dismantled during the Civil War to clear the field of fire, then rebuilt towards the close of the 17th century. It is first referred to as an inn in 1775 and was run by the family of Samuel Guest until 1826, whereafter it changed hands frequently. The inn finally closed in the 1960s and was later demolished. Rutter's garage is now on the site.

142 8 Pound Street with Mrs. H. Rogers in 1904. It was demolished in 1940 after suffering serious damage when a lone enemy plane dropped a string of bombs on Bridgnorth.

143 The *Carpenter's Arms*, Whitburn Street, *c*.1895. First licensed in 1840, this was built as a private dwelling long before the houses on the opposite side of the road. The demolition of the Whitburn Gate in 1761 entailed the lowering of the road surface, thus leaving the houses already built needing steps for access. These steps now encroach onto the pavements that were narrowed when Whitburn Street was widened for 20th-century traffic.

144 Whitburn Street in the late 1870s. On the left-hand side, only the square bay over the back entrance to the *King's Head* and the two adjoining shops remain. The *Pheasant Inn*, on the corner of the High Street and the adjoining house were demolished and replaced by the Worcester City and County Bank in 1879. The next property, too, is part of the present Lloyds Bank. Opposite is the *Raven*. The date sign, now between the two corbels on the right of the door, was not there! The *Crown and Cushion* at the end of the street became Jeffries cycle shop in 1895. Since the war, the building has been refronted in brick.

145 The tablet beneath the window of the *Raven* in 1939. There have been suggestions that it was recovered from the debris of the town and used in the rebuilding of the *Raven*. It is still the subject of much speculation.

146 The town's only late Victorian shop, built flamboyantly in 1892 with each floor in a different style, overshadows its neighbours. On the left is the late 16th-century grocer's shop and on the right the 17th-century timber-framed *King's Head Hotel*. Joseph Weaver managed the tea warehouse and acted as an agent for Gilbey's.

147 This house behind Whitburn Street was used as a police house. Chief Constable Cole lived there until 1887 as head of the Borough's own police force. Two cells remain at the back of the house, each with a studded oak door, padlock and chain. The gaol house (approached from the Northgate) which joined this property was pulled down in 1923. A House of Correction was recorded on its site in 1654.

148 A crowd of townsfolk look on in 1875 during a recruiting drive. Two children on the left-hand pavement keep their distance from John Cole, Chief Constable of Bridgnorth.

149 'F' (Bridgnorth) Company 1st Volunteer Battalion, King's Shropshire Light Infantry approach Northgate under the command of Lieutenant William Westcott in 1898. Note one very young member of the band!

150 *Left*. The Northgate *c.*1875. In 1740 this building had replaced an ancient gatehouse which had been converted into a prison in 1638. The 30 boys of the Blue Coat School were housed in the Burgesses' Hall above the Northgate from 1719 to 1910. The rough street outside that gate was their playground until the provision of the Innage recreation ground in 1886. The ground floor of the adjoining building was converted into the fire station in 1879.

151 *Bottom left*. The firecrew and equipment pose proudly in front of their new fire station opened in 1879. On the left, timber-framed houses 3 and 4 High Street were amongst the few properties in High Town that escaped the Civil War fires.

152 In 1888 a regularly organised fire brigade was established using a horse-drawn steam fire engine. In 1893, when further assistance was required for a fire at the carpet works, messengers were dispatched on horseback to Claverley, Shifnal and the Maws tile works at Jackfield. Left to right: (back row) G. Crockson, W. Preen, W. Dexter, S. Wright, C. Massey, W. Owen (Captain); (front row) J. Thomas, E. Langford, S. Jordan, J. Lester, H. Bishop, W. Thomas, - Childs (Superintendent).

153 *Left*. This steam fire engine, pulled by the Corporation lorry, was in use until 1937.

154 *Bottom left*. The first motor-driven fire engine, attracting the residents of Riverside in 1937.

155 The Northgate, *c*.1875. The signboard over the small arch was a relic of coaching days. The door to the left of the arch led into a gentlemen's lavatory until the present walkway was made in the 1940s. The small window on the right formerly looked out from a small prison (the 'Thieves Hole', which housed the whipping post).

156 Samuel Instone, seen here in his bowler hat, kept the shop adjoining Northgate. The front ground floor of the building was removed in 1909 to make a way through the third arch of the gate which was opened in 1910. Instone's butcher's shop, from that date until 1922, was at 1 St Mary's Street.

157 Mr. and Mrs. Joshua Newsome photographed outside the old gaol.

158 In 1967 the new fire station was opened on Innage Lane. Left to right: LFM G. Newsome, LFM D. Blount, FM P. Hulland, FM F. Prince, FM D. Hulme, FM T. Winwood, FM L. Winwood, Station Officer C. Markie, FM R. Groom, Sub Officer H. Jones, LFM R. Dudgon, FM A. Thompson, FM B. Bowen, FM L. Owen, FM R. Lloyd, FM E. Winwood.

159 Mineral water was produced in Moat Street from 1888 until the early 1960s for many years under the management of Mr. G. 'Pop' Jones. This early photograph was taken from the back entrance in Cliff Road. Mr. Watkiss has been identified as one of the men.

160 In 1886 a special cycle track was laid out on the cricket field in Love Lane. Bank Holiday sports included athletics, aquatic and cycling events and horse, Galloway and pony races. A military band played from the bandstand. Dunval House can be seen in the background. Amongst those in the photograph can be recognised: W. Jones (Waterloo House), F. Callant (Gas Works Manager), C.H. Cunnington (headmaster of the Blue Coat School), H. Gadsby (jeweller's shop), C. Brawn (shop), J. Matthews, D. Broadbent.

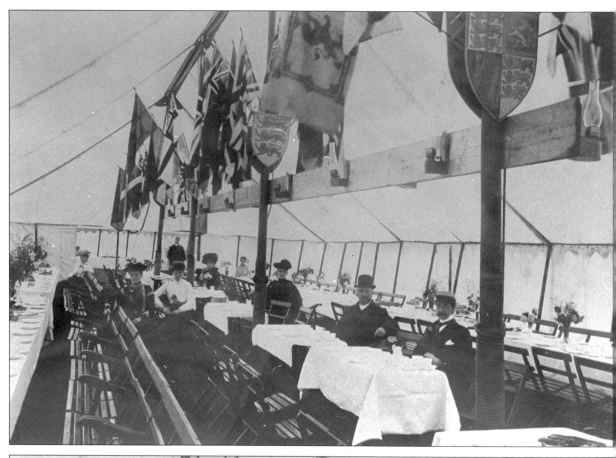
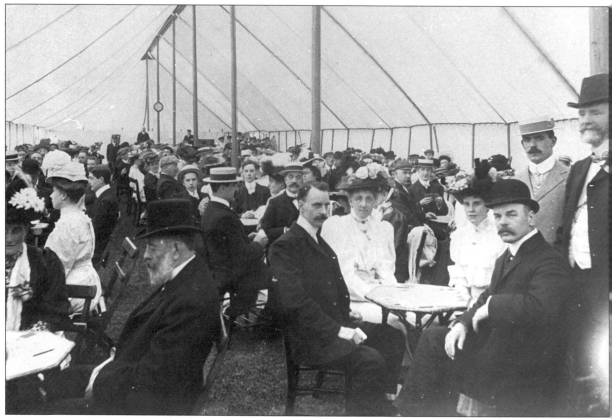

161 *Left.* The tea tent on Love Lane Sports Ground. Annual sports were held in August, with competitors coming from all over the Midlands. Events ranged from 100 yards foot races to two-mile cycle events. In the Diamond Jubilee year, 1897, 4,000 spectators lined the track and there were 359 entrants.

162 *Bottom left.* A whist drive held in the marquee on the athletics ground, Love Lane, *c.*1900. Mr. William Jones of Waterloo House, standing on the rostrum, was the captain of the Cycling Club.

163 Bridgnorth Guides in 1925. Left to right: (back row) Connie Hathaway, Elsie Preece, Bessie Tranter, Edna Rudd; (middle row) Barbara Route, Elsie Winwood, 'Pop' Perry, Miss Baynley (Captain); (front row) Gladys Gough, Jessie Preece, May Tench, Katy Shaw.

164 Tanks in the High Street in May 1937. The 33rd Field Brigade Royal Artillery were on a recruiting drive.

165 *Above right.* Sandbags protecting the police station in Whitburn Street, November 1939.

166 *Right.* National Savings Week, May 1944. Spectators were keen to see savings rise towards the £200,000 target. Earle's ironmonger's was a selling centre.

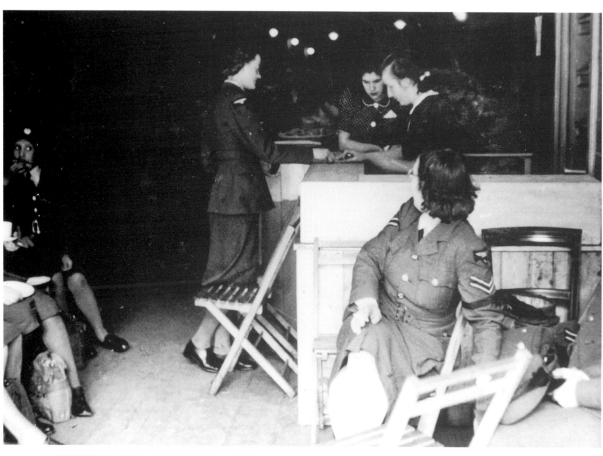

167 *Left.* 73 High Street, Bridgnorth Garage, was used as a Toc-H canteen in wartime. It became Bees Snack Bar from 1947-60.

168 *Bottom left.* Bridgnorth Women's Junior Air Corps parading in Mill Street in 1943. Their C.O. was Betty Fearnley, a physics teacher at the Grammar School.

169 The 8th Shropshire Battalion, Home Guard Stand-Down Parade 3 December 1944 led by C.O. Major Nicholas. The salute was taken by Lt. Col. R.W. Wilson.

170 *Left*. The Roden family with American servicemen
Cpl. Brantley and Staff Sgt. Davidson at the war memorial
in 1944.

171   The site of the bomb-damaged houses in Pound Street, cleared by 1944.

172 *Left.* A party of children waiting for their coach to Dudley Zoo, a treat organised to celebrate V.E. Day, May 1945.

173 *Bottom left.* Roden's grocer's shop, 72 High Street in April 1945. From the left: Doreen Gower, Freda Bache and Sylvia Roden serving a very limited range of groceries! Jam, rationed on 'points', was made from local fruit by the Women's Voluntary Service.

174 A children's party under the Town Hall on 23 August 1945 in celebration of V.J. Day.

Bibliography

Anderson, J.C., *Shropshire: Its Early History and Antiquities* (1864)
Baker, J., *Nock Deighton and Son* (1981)
Bellett, G., *The Antiquities of Bridgnorth* (1856)
Deighton, *Bridgnorth Almanack* (1896, 1911)
Duke, T.F., *Antiquities of Shropshire* (1844)
Dyas Collection, Shropshire Record Office 796/95-96
Elliott, D.J., *Policing Shropshire 1836-1967* (1984)
Fothergill, C., *Bridgnorth Journal* (various)
Hamilton-Ellis, *The Love of the Train* (1971)
Head, F., *Weaving in Bridgnorth* (1941)
Mason, J.F.A., *Bridgnorth Borough Arms* (1959)
Mason, J.F.A., *The Borough of Bridgnorth 1157-1957* (1957)
Morris, R.K., *The Shropshire Severn* (1994)
Randall, J., *Tourist Guide to Bridgnorth* (1875)
Shropshire Archaeological Society, *Transactions*, 1st series, vol. x, vol. xi
Smith, D.J., *The Severn Valley Railway* (1968)
Smith, H., *Tent Life with English Gypsies in Norway* (1873)
Thomas, J.M. Lloyd, *Autobiography of Richard Baxter* (1925)
Toghill, P., *Geology of Shropshire* (1990)
Trinder, B., *The Industrial Revolution in Shropshire* (1973)
Wanklyn, M., 'Bridgnorth and the River Trade 1660-1800', *Midland History* (1994)
Watkins-Pitchford, W., *High Town Tour* (1939)
Watkins-Pitchford, W., *The Port of Bridgnorth* (1935)

Index

Roman numerals refer to pages in the introduction, and arabic numerals to individual illustrations.

Etching by S. and N. Buck of Bridgnorth from the south west, 1732, the earliest known engraving of the town. Note the bowling green by the castle.